AF596803

# *Thank You* CREATOR

***The Ultimate Gratitude Handbook***

JEYASREE RAVI

INDIA • SINGAPORE • MALAYSIA

Copyright © Jeyasree Ravi 2025
All Rights Reserved.

ISBN
Paperback 979-8-88869-950-8
Hardcase 979-8-89699-376-6

This book has been published with all efforts taken to make the material error-free after the consent of the author. However, the author and the publisher do not assume and hereby disclaim any liability to any party for any loss, damage, or disruption caused by errors or omissions, whether such errors or omissions result from negligence, accident, or any other cause.

While every effort has been made to avoid any mistake or omission, this publication is being sold on the condition and understanding that neither the author nor the publishers or printers would be liable in any manner to any person by reason of any mistake or omission in this publication or for any action taken or omitted to be taken or advice rendered or accepted on the basis of this work. For any defect in printing or binding the publishers will be liable only to replace the defective copy by another copy of this work then available.

# Why Should You Read This Book?

Find answers to the questions

that twirl around you...

Find ways to reach your goal...

Quicker & Faster...

More than making amends in your life,

Stand tall as an example to

lead a righteous life...

# What Happens When You Truly Praise the Creator?

- Your seven chakras will be aligned to the Universal energy and you and your soul will become a part of the divine cosmos.
- You will be able to pick up the reins of your life and every decision or step you take in your life will be as per the divine paradigm.
- You will be truly content with your life as our Creator will hold your hands and walk with you.

# My Experience with Thank You Creator…

For the past few years, I have been reading this book every day. I had a minor hormonal disorder, and I started reading the book twice a day. I believed the words in this book would heal me. When I say I read it, I mean I read the whole book. Initially, I was just reading it, but not mindfully. When India went into a nationwide lockdown in the wake of the pandemic, I had more time in hand. I started reading it at a much slower pace, which allowed me to enjoy every single line assimilating the meaning of every single word. I could sense a feeling of pure happiness, a kind of happiness that I had not sensed before in my life. I continued reading this book twice a day, first thing in the morning and in the evening.

As lockdown restrictions were lifted and I got back to work, I continued reading it in the morning. Just reading it made me feel good. Sometimes I wrote a prayer and read the prayer after every page. I continued the prayer for a few weeks. And then I reverted to just reading the lines, feeling grateful, without any particular prayer to recite.

As I continued reading, I did not realise the change in me. It happened gradually over a span of 3 or 4 years that I hardly noticed it, and not until my friends and acquaintances pointed it out to me. I seemed to have noticeably become calm. Something that I had not realized myself.

As people started mentioning this to me, I began to consciously notice the changes within. When things went wrong, I was able to handle them better. I did lose my temper on a few occasions, but I was able to regain my calm and balance quite quickly.

How did this happen? The only change in my routine was reading this book. It was the one thing that I had been consistent with—reading this book, the whole book, every single day. I'm unable to attribute the change in me to anything other than this.

Each person's experience with this book is likely to be different. Read it consistently to experience it. The calm that it creates within is addictive; you will effortlessly find yourself gravitating to that state. You will be able to feel and experience pure bliss throughout the day, almost effortlessly. You will find that it has become your natural state of being eventually.

Thank You, Creator!

# Prayers to the Creator

# Daily Prayer

Thank you Creator for giving us this life,

Food, Clothing, and Shelter

Let the Peace You have given me

make others find peace in You...

Let Your love as shown to others

Make others love you...

Let Your forgiving nature

Make us forgive each other...

Let Your nature of equality

Through all creations be seen by us...

Let the faith and trust I have in you

Make others have faith and trust in you...

To You Creator, who removes sufferings

And blesses with happiness

We, the creations proudly belong.

# Forgiveness Prayer

Bless me Lord, our Creator

To realise, repent and

Ask forgiveness for all my mistakes,

To live by the path of Truth and

Chastity, as You will

All praises to You Creator

# Welfare Prayer

Lord, our Creator

Bless my family with peace and serenity

Bless us all to lead an immaculate and a

truthful life,

In Accordance with Your will.

Bless us with the knowledge,

Intelligence and mindset to understand

Your will and do as You will,

To follow the path of truth, to enjoy eternal bliss.

# How to Meditate/Pray?

- First, completely believe that you deserve to connect with the Universal energy.
- You must feel happy and grateful when you read the book. No Tears, No Complaints. You may read this book anytime, anywhere.
- List out all your requests you wish to put forth to the Creator and add the Forgiveness and Welfare Prayer as well.
- Prioritize all your prayers and keep aside a prayer for each day.
- Look at a line
- Close your eyes and repeat the line in your mind understanding the meaning and go to the next line and so on.
- When you reach the end of each page, feel the happiness and gratitude for 10 seconds.
- Say your prayer for the day.
- Again, feel the happiness and gratitude for 10 seconds.

Proceed to the next page IMMEDIATELY.

# This is Meditation

- Practice this daily and BE CONSISTENT.
- Begin with 3 to 5 pages and try to increase the number of pages gradually.
- If you read the full book every day for 30 days with the forgiveness prayer, you will be able to erase your Karma and heal yourself for real.

# Thank You Creator

Thank You Creator, The Greatest of all creations

Thank You Creator, The Omnipotent

Thank You Creator, The Most Powerful

Thank You Creator, The Righteous

Thank You Creator, The Awesome

Thank You Creator, The Precious

Thank You Creator, The Sanctifier

Thank You Creator, The One who is present

Thank You Creator, The Healer

Thank You Creator, Our Righteousness

Thank You Creator, The Provider

Thank You Creator, Our Banner

Thank You Creator, The Source of Peace

Thank You Creator, The Lord of Hosts

Thank You Creator, The God of Recompense

Thank You Creator, The Highest God

Thank You Creator, The Strong One who sees

Thank You Creator, The God of the Mountains

Thank You Creator, God Almighty

Thank You Creator, The Everlasting God

Thank You Creator, God, our Father

Thank You Creator, My Deliverer

Thank You Creator, The Holy Father, the Self, the One, I AM.

Thank You Creator, Lord of Lords

Thank You Creator, Lord of Glory

Thank You Creator, My Strength

Thank You Creator, The Highest

Thank You Creator, Our Defence

Thank You Creator, My Redeemer

Thank You Creator, The King

Thank You Creator, My Judge

Thank You Creator, The King forever

Thank You Creator, The Saviour

Thank You Creator, The Consciousness in all living things

Thank You Creator, My Glory

Thank You Creator, The Lord of Salvation

Thank You Creator, My Refuge

Thank You Creator, My Shield

Thank You Creator, My Fortress

Thank You Creator, My Rock

Thank You Creator, My Light

Thank You Creator, My Strength in trouble

Thank You Creator, The Lord who said "I am that I am"

Thank You Creator, The Most Powerful

Thank You Creator, The Beginning and The End

Thank You Creator, The Cause of all creation

Thank You Creator, The Lord of Paradise

Thank You Creator, The Merciful

Thank You Creator, The Compassionate

Thank You Creator, The Supreme

Thank You Creator, The Affirmer of truth

Thank You Creator, The Gracious

Thank You Creator, The Holy

Thank You Creator, The Pure

Thank You Creator, The Guardian

Thank You Creator, The Honourable

Thank You Creator, The Majestic

Thank You Creator, The Lord of Forgiveness

Thank You Creator, The Bestower

Thank You Creator, The All-Knowing

Thank You Creator, The Omniscient

Thank You Creator, The Artisan of artisans

Thank You Creator, The Giver of Honour

Thank You Creator, The Just

Thank You Creator, The Magnificent

Thank You Creator, The Much Forgiving

Thank You Creator, The Great

Thank You Creator, The Preserver

Thank You Creator, The One who nourishes

Thank You Creator, The All-Embracing

Thank You Creator, The Watchful

Thank You Creator, Our Caretaker

Thank You Creator, The One without Origin

Thank You Creator, The All-Glorious

Thank You Creator, The Truth

Thank You Creator, The Trustee

Thank You Creator, The Dependable

Thank You Creator, The Strong

Thank You Creator, The Advocate

Thank You Creator, The Firm

Thank You Creator, The Steadfast

Thank You Creator, Our Friend

Thank You Creator, The All Praiseworthy

Thank You Creator, The Originator

Thank You Creator, The Producer

Thank You Creator, The Initiator

Thank You Creator, The Restorer

Thank You Creator, The Giver of life

Thank You Creator, The Unfailing

Thank You Creator, The Unity

Thank You Creator, The Indivisible

Thank You Creator, He in whom there is no harm

Thank You Creator, The Absolute

Thank You Creator, The All Able

Thank You Creator, The Determiner

Thank You Creator, The Dominant

Thank You Creator, The Expediter

Thank You Creator, The First

Thank You Creator, The Beginningless

Thank You Creator, The Last

Thank You Creator, The Endless

Thank You Creator, The Manifest

Thank You Creator, The Unmanifest

Thank You Creator, The Kind

Thank You Creator, The Pitying

Thank You Creator, The Ultimate Source of Peace

Thank You Creator, The Unifier

Thank You Creator, The Independent

Thank You Creator, The Emancipator

Thank You Creator, The Defender

Thank You Creator, The Guide

Thank You Creator, The Way

Thank You Creator, The Immutable

Thank You Creator, The Infinite

Thank You Creator, The Everlasting

Thank You Creator, The Patient

Thank You Creator, The Timeless

Thank You Creator, The Ever Victorious

Thank You Creator, The Lord of Heaven

Thank You Creator, The Cause of the Universe

Thank You Creator, The Supreme Controller

Thank You Creator, The Master of all things - past, present and future

Thank You Creator, The Supporter of all things

Thank You Creator, The Splendorous

Thank You Creator, The Soul of all beings

Thank You Creator, The Supreme Soul

Thank You Creator, The Nurturer of all things

Thank You Creator, The Pure Self

Thank You Creator, The Indestructible

Thank You Creator, The All-Knower

Thank You Creator, The Supreme Bliss

Thank You Creator, The Primordial Force

Thank You Creator, The Remover of all sins

Thank You Creator, The One who Bestows Bountiful Blessings

Thank You Creator, The Inexhaustible Treasure

Thank You Creator, The Unchanging

Thank You Creator, The Eternal Self

Thank You Creator, The Embodiment of Supreme Auspiciousness

Thank You Creator, The Most Praiseworthy

Thank You Creator, Lord of the Angels

Thank You Creator, The Most Courageous

Thank You Creator, The All-Seeing

Thank You Creator, The Unborn

Thank You Creator, The Remover of all obstacles

Thank You Creator, The Remover of ignorance

Thank You Creator, The Origin

Thank You Creator, The Incomprehensible

Thank You Creator, The One who lives in our hearts

Thank You Creator, The One to whom all are equal

Thank You Creator, The Immortal

Thank You Creator, The One who is eternally firm

Thank You Creator, The One of excellent ascent

Thank You Creator, The Perfect

Thank You Creator, The Forgiver

Thank You Creator, The Sinless

Thank You Creator, The Conqueror

Thank You Creator, The Supreme light

Thank You Creator, The Leader of the hosts of angels

Thank You Creator, The Radiant

Thank You Creator, The Soul of the Universe

Thank You Creator, The Essence of Life

Thank You Creator, The Dispeller of darkness

Thank You Creator, The Giver of Life-breath

Thank You Creator, The Incomparable

Thank You Creator, The Giver of wealth

Thank You Creator, The Restorer

Thank You Creator, The Most Bounteous Spirit

Thank You Creator, The Most Lovable

Thank You Creator, The Most Loving

Thank You Creator, The Impartial

Thank You Creator, The Supporter of the Universe

Thank You Creator, The Life Breath

Thank You Creator, The Dispeller of sorrows

Thank You Creator, The Valiant

Thank You Creator, The Formidable

Thank You Creator, The Ultimate Truth

Thank You Creator, The Remover of bondage

Thank You Creator, The Supreme Ruler

Thank You Creator, The Pivot of the worlds

Thank You Creator, The Giver of Supreme abode

Thank You Creator, The Faultless

Thank You Creator, The Virtue Incarnate

Thank You Creator, The Purifier

Thank You Creator, The Lord of time

Thank You Creator, The Supreme Authority

Thank You Creator, The Greatest Treasure

Thank You Creator, The All-Supporter

Thank You Creator, The Bestower of Bliss

Thank You Creator, The All-pervading

Thank You Creator, The Most Affectionate

Thank You Creator, The Protector of Truth

Thank You Creator, The Most Commendable

Thank You Creator, The Rescuer

Thank You Creator, Source of all Knowledge

Thank You Creator, The Observer

Thank You Creator, The Only One worthy of Worship

Thank You Creator, The Impenetrable

Thank You Creator, The Inexplicable

Thank You Creator, The Intelligence in all beings

Thank You Creator, The Doer

Thank You Creator, The Bountiful

Thank You Creator, The All-Inclusive

Thank You Creator, The Maker

Thank You Creator, The Most Kind

Thank You Creator, The Forbearing

Thank You Creator, The Limitless

Thank You Creator, The All-Aware

Thank You Creator, The Sovereign

Thank You Creator, The Defender

Thank You Creator, The Protecting Friend, Patron, and Helper

Thank You Creator, The Illustrious

Thank You Creator, The Enriched

Thank You Creator, The Sustainer

Thank You Creator, The Equitable

Thank You Creator, The Self Exalted

Thank You Creator, The Propitious

Thank You Creator, The Benefactor

Thank You Creator, The Compassionate

Thank You Creator, The Bestower of Peace

Thank You Creator, The Self Sufficient

Thank You Creator, The Bestower of Intelligence

Thank You Creator, The Most Noble

Thank You Creator, The Most Excellent

Thank You Creator, The One without any blemish

Thank You Creator, The Best Instructor on the path of Truth

Thank You Creator, The Resplendent

Thank You Creator, The Most Complete

Thank You Creator, The Fulfiller of Desires

Thank You Creator, The Giver of treasure

Thank You Creator, The Giver of glory

Thank You Creator, The Most Adorable

Thank You Creator, The Dweller in our hearts

Thank You Creator, Who is attainable by the pure

Thank You Creator, The Supreme Goal of the pure

Thank You Creator, The Invincible

Thank You Creator, Who is Matchless in all respects

Thank You Creator, The Unexcelled Protector

Thank You Creator, The Supreme Goal

Thank You Creator, The Object of Honour

Thank You Creator, The Blessed

Thank You Creator, The Well Intentioned

Thank You Creator, The Subduer

Thank You Creator, The Dispeller of evil thoughts

Thank You Creator, The Most Auspicious

Thank You Creator, The One who bestows knowledge of the Supreme Reality

Thank You Creator, The Unconstrained

Thank You Creator, The Unsustained

Thank You Creator, The Dispeller of Miseries

Thank You Creator, The Imperishable Power

Thank You Creator, The Law Maker, The Law Giver

Thank You Creator, The Most Luminous

Thank You Creator, The Enjoyer of Bliss

Thank You Creator, The Lord beyond words

Thank You Creator, The Lord of Inviolable laws

Thank You Creator, The Most Charming

Thank You Creator, The Most Pleasing

Thank You Creator, The Most Amiable

Thank You Creator, The Best

Thank You Creator, The Foremost

Thank You Creator, The Dispeller of fear

Thank You Creator, The Most Precious

Thank You Creator, The Law

Thank You Creator, The Vital Source

Thank You Creator, The Supreme Manager of the Universe

Thank You Creator, The Pure Infinite Consciousness

Thank You Creator, The Reality

Thank You Creator, The Nature Divine

Thank You Creator, The Absolute Self

Thank You Creator, The Ever Peaceful

Thank You Creator, The Lord of Infinite Patience

Thank You Creator, The Author of Life

Thank You Creator, The Author of Peace

Thank You Creator, The Most Wonderful

Thank You Creator, The Author of Miracles

Thank You Creator, The Most Marvellous

Thank You Creator, The Higher than the highest

Thank You Creator, The Perfect in Knowledge

Thank You Creator, The Majesty on High

Thank You Creator, The Most Upright

Thank You Creator, My Refuge

Thank You Creator, My Trust

Thank You Creator, My Comforter

Thank You Creator, The Lord of Wisdom

Thank You Creator, The Absolute Existence, Consciousness, and Bliss

Thank You Creator, The Possessor of Innumerable Virtues

Thank You Creator, The Supreme

Thank You Creator, The Stable

Thank You Creator, The Possessor of Inconceivable Powers

Thank You Creator, The Subtle

Thank You Creator, The Bestower of Divine love

Thank You Creator, The One beyond reach

Thank You Creator, The Unequalled

Thank You Creator, The Most Generous

Thank You Creator, The Imperceptible

Thank You Creator, The One who gives infinite happiness

Thank You Creator, The One who gives food and clothing

Thank You Creator, The Guardian of the helpless

Thank You Creator, The Indweller in all

Thank You Creator, The One who gives Grace

Thank You Creator, The One with immeasurable strength

Thank You Creator, The Formless

Thank You Creator, The Invisible

Thank You Creator, The Inexhaustible

Thank You Creator, The One without impossibilities

Thank You Creator, The Unshakeable

Thank You Creator, The Destroyer of ignorance

Thank You Creator, The Destroyer of ego

Thank You Creator, The Remover of afflictions

Thank You Creator, The Primal Energy

Thank You Creator, The very Foundation of Power

Thank You Creator, The One who is Bliss

Thank You Creator, The Destroyer of calamities

Thank You Creator, The Spiritual Guide

Thank You Creator, The One beyond bounds

Thank You Creator, The Liberator

Thank You Creator, The One and Only

Thank You Creator, The Destroyer of the evils of sins

Thank You Creator, The Remover of impurities

Thank You Creator, The Embodiment of compassion

Thank You Creator, The Treasure of mercy

Thank You Creator, The Mine of compassion

Thank You Creator, The One who suppresses the evil

Thank You Creator, The One beyond attributes

Thank You Creator, The Mysterious

Thank You Creator, The Triumphant, the Victorious

Thank You Creator, The Illuminator

Thank You Creator, The Supreme Spirit

Thank You Creator, The Treasure of Brilliance

Thank You Creator, The One who is fond of charity

Thank You Creator, The All-Encompassing

Thank You Creator, The Fearless

Thank You Creator, The Embodiment of Purity

Thank You Creator, The Most Sacred

Thank You Creator, The Benevolent

Thank You Creator, The Most Evident

Thank You Creator, The Most Gracious

Thank You Creator, The Destroyer of illusion

Thank You Creator, The Destroyer of delusion

Thank You Creator, The Goal of the truthful

Thank You Creator, The Eternal Guide

Thank You Creator, The Impartial

Thank You Creator, The Universal Monarch

Thank You Creator, The Embodiment of Knowledge

Thank You Creator, The Most Effulgent

Thank You Creator, The Bestower of success

Thank You Creator, The Remover of the fear of evil

Thank You Creator, The Supreme Principle

Thank You Creator, The Upholder of the worlds

Thank You Creator, The Eternal comfort

Thank You Creator, The Supreme Happiness

Thank You Creator, The Supreme Security

Thank You Creator, The Ultimate Realization

Thank You Creator, The One who possesses infinite Auspicious Attributes

Thank You Creator, The Epitome of all Virtues

Thank You Creator, The One who possesses limitless Powers

Thank You Creator, The Unconquerable

Thank You Creator, The Personification of Subtlety

Thank You Creator, The Performer of Infinite Miracles

Thank You Creator, The Bestower of all auspicious Grace

Thank You Creator, The Source of Intuition

Thank You Creator, The Immeasurable

Thank You Creator, The One who is unbiased

Thank You Creator, My Anchor

Thank You Creator, My Assurance

Thank You Creator, The Indescribable

Thank You Creator, The Uncontainable

Thank You Creator, The Amazing

Thank You Creator, The Sovereign

Thank You Creator, The Self-existent

Thank You Creator, The Impassable

Thank You Creator, The All-Wise

Thank You Creator, The Omnipresent

Thank You Creator, The All-knowing

Thank You Creator, The One who sanctifies you

Thank You Creator, The Embodiment of Goodness

Thank You Creator, The Embodiment of Integrity

Thank You Creator, The Perfectly Benevolent

Thank You Creator, The Perfectly Trustworthy

Thank You Creator, The Source of Salvation

Thank You Creator, The Perfect One with Unchanging Wisdom

Thank You Creator, The Mysterious

Thank You Creator, The Promise Keeper

Thank You Creator, The Lord of Absolute Faithfulness

Thank You Creator, The Lord of Unlimited Energy

Thank You Creator, The Most Worthy

Thank You Creator, My Hope

Thank You Creator, The Ruler of the Universe

Thank You Creator, The Responsive, the Answerer

Thank You Creator, My Restorer

Thank You Creator, My Stronghold in the day of trouble

Thank You Creator, My Resting Place

Thank You Creator, The Light of the world

Thank You Creator, My Refiner

Thank You Creator, My Refuge from the storm

Thank You Creator, My Overcomer

Thank You Creator, The Bread of life

Thank You Creator, My Fortress

Thank You Creator, My Rewarder

Thank You Creator, The Author of my Faith

Thank You Creator, My Everlasting Father

Thank You Creator, The One who loves unconditionally

Thank You Creator, The Transcendent

Thank You Creator, The Unfathomable

Thank You Creator, The One who is ever consistent

Thank You Creator, The One whose love is never-ending

Thank You Creator, The Lord of Enduring Faithfulness

Thank You Creator, The One who forgives the repentant

Thank You Creator, The One who is Solitary

Thank You Creator, The Unique

Thank You Creator, The One without equal

Thank You Creator, The Only One worthy of submission

Thank You Creator, The Most Esteemed

Thank You Creator, My Supreme Companion

Thank You Creator, The Invincible

Thank You Creator, The One who is the Master of all virtues

Thank You Creator, The Vanquisher of all evils, vices and sins

Thank You Creator, The Repository of Compassion

Thank You Creator, The LORD of all senses

Thank You Creator, The LORD of Brilliance

Thank You Creator, The Boundless

Thank You Creator, The Most Sacred

Thank You Creator, The Inconceivable

Thank You Creator, The Incredible

Thank You Creator, The Most Exalted

Thank You Creator, Splendiferous

Thank You Creator, The Most August

Thank You Creator, The Most Venerable

Thank You Creator, The Monumental

Thank You Creator, The Grand

Thank You Creator, The Stupendous

Thank You Creator, The Tremendous

Thank You Creator, The Wondrous

Thank You Creator, The One with overwhelming Power

Thank You Creator, The Most Glorious

Thank You Creator, The Magnanimous

Thank You Creator, The Superb

Thank You Creator, The Supreme Ultimate Reality

Thank You Creator, The Unrivalled

Thank You Creator, The Unparalleled

Thank You Creator, The Consummate

Thank You Creator, The Unmatchable

Thank You Creator, The Fantastic

Thank You Creator, The Unsurpassable

Thank You Creator, The Paramount

Thank You Creator, The Predominant

Thank You Creator, The Inimitable

Thank You Creator, The Impeccable

Thank You Creator, The Immaculate

Thank You Creator, The Unexceptionable

Thank You Creator, The Genuine

Thank You Creator, The Most Honourable

Thank You Creator, The Perfect One with unchanging wisdom

Thank You Creator, The Miraculous

Thank You Creator, The Peerless

Thank You Creator, The Inexplicable

Thank You Creator, The Matchless

Thank You Creator, The Exemplary

Thank You Creator, The Unprecedented

Thank You Creator, The Pre-eminent

Thank You Creator, The Terrific

Thank You Creator, The Paradisiacal

Thank You Creator, The Indestructible

Thank You Creator, The Abundant

Thank You Creator, The Most Commendable

Thank You Creator, The Insurmountable

Thank You Creator, The Insuperable

Thank You Creator, The Untainted

Thank You Creator, The One whose Greatness never diminishes

Thank You Creator, The One who alone is the unobstructed means to salvation

Thank You Creator, The Lord of Primordial Matter

Thank You Creator, The Indefinable

Thank You Creator, The One who has always existed

Thank You Creator, The Controller

Thank You Creator, The Pardoner, The Effacer of sins

Thank You Creator, The Basis for order in the Universe

Thank You Creator, The Embodiment of Truth

Thank You Creator, The Effulgent One

Thank You Creator, The Uncontaminated One

Thank You Creator, The Victory Incarnate

Thank You Creator, The One with immeasurable strength

Thank You Creator, The Most Enchanting

Thank You Creator, The One of great virility

Thank You Creator, The Ultimate Goal of all spiritual seekers

Thank You Creator, The Unassailable

Thank You Creator, The Imperishable

Thank You Creator, The One with innumerable attributes

Thank You Creator, The One who showers Grace in Abundance

Thank You Creator, The One who pervades everything

Thank You Creator, The Grantor of wishes

Thank You Creator, The Uncompromising

Thank You Creator, The One of multifarious wonders

Thank You Creator, The Owner and Controller of souls

Thank You Creator, The Seed of the Universe

Thank You Creator, The All-Seeing

Thank You Creator, The All-Knower

Thank You Creator, The One of incomprehensible nature

Thank You Creator, The Wise

Thank You Creator, The Controller of the affairs of the cosmos

Thank You Creator, The One whose will prevails

Thank You Creator, The One whose Greatness is explicit

Thank You Creator, The Vital Air

Thank You Creator, The Goal of the pious

Thank You Creator, The One who resides in the Supreme Abode

Thank You Creator, The Seed Imperishable

Thank You Creator, The Alpha and the Omega

Thank You Creator, The Dispeller of all doubts

Thank You Creator, The Restrainer of lawlessness

Thank You Creator, The Valiant

Thank You Creator, The One who permeates everything—sentient and non-sentient

Thank You Creator, The One who controls and directs

Thank You Creator, The One who nourishes and nurtures all beings He created

Thank You Creator, The One who directly witnesses everything as it is

Thank You Creator, The One who leads us to Supreme Bliss

Thank You Creator, The Unchanging and Permanent

Thank You Creator, The One who never forsakes anyone

Thank You Creator, The One who is the Wealth that we seek

Thank You Creator, The unstinting Nectar to Your seekers

Thank You Creator, The One who is the Most Supreme Object of attainment

Thank You Creator, The One who is full of all Glories

Thank You Creator, The One who controls all movements in beings

Thank You Creator, The One who controls the movement of all celestial bodies

Thank You Creator, The Lord of Retribution

Thank You Creator, The Self Subsisting

Thank You Creator, The Exalted in Might

Thank You Creator, The Grantor of bounties without measure

Thank You Creator, The All-pervading hidden Essence

Thank You Creator, The Knowledge itself

Thank You Creator, The Source of Truth

Thank You Creator, The Beloved

Thank You Creator, The All glorious Ruler of the universe

Thank You Creator, The Knower of the unseen and the visible

Thank You Creator, The All-Holy

Thank You Creator, The Guardian of Faith

Thank You Creator, The All-Compelled

Thank You Creator, The All-Sublime

Thank You Creator, The All-High

Thank You Creator, The Source of Peace

Thank You Creator, The Overpowering

Thank You Creator, The  Inscrutable Power in all beings

Thank You Creator, The Decider

Thank You Creator, The Withholder

Thank You Creator, The Plentiful Giver

Thank You Creator, The Perfect One with unchanging wisdom

Thank You Creator, The Exalted

Thank You Creator, The Clement

Thank You Creator, The One who Rewards

Thank You Creator, The Guide, the Infallible
Teacher, the Knower

Thank You Creator, The Generous

Thank You Creator, The Watcher

Thank You Creator, The Answerer

Thank You Creator, The Liberal

Thank You Creator, The Wise

Thank You Creator, The Witness

Thank You Creator, The Real

Thank You Creator, The One to whom men repent

Thank You Creator, The Advancer

Thank You Creator, The Delayer

Thank You Creator, The Faithful

Thank You Creator, The Infinitely, Unchangingly True

Thank You Creator, The Giver of prosperity

Thank You Creator, The Patron

Thank You Creator, The Governor

Thank You Creator, The Acceptor of repentance

Thank You Creator, The Upholder of truth, justice and order

Thank You Creator, The Pardoner

Thank You Creator, The Kind-hearted

Thank You Creator, The One who enriches

Thank You Creator, Your Decree shall ever stand

Thank You Creator, The One with understanding

Thank You Creator, The Noble

Thank You Creator, The Non-dual

Thank You Creator, The Lord beyond comparison

Thank You Creator, The Lord beyond imagination and conception

Thank You Creator, The One who always was, always is, and always will be

Thank You Creator, The One who is everywhere, in everything

Thank You Creator, The One beyond everywhere and beyond everything

Thank You Creator, The One on all planes and beyond the planes

Thank You Creator, The Knower of all minds and hearts

Thank You Creator, The Trinity of Truth, Knowledge, and Bliss

Thank You Creator, The Ancient One

Thank You Creator, The Ocean of Love

Thank You Creator, The Highest of the high

Thank You Creator, The One who has plenty of mercy for the believers

Thank You Creator, The Compeller and the One without whose will nothing happens

Thank You Creator, The One who lowers whoever He willed

Thank You Creator, The One who raises whoever He willed by His Endowment

Thank You Creator, The One who gives esteem to whoever He willed

Thank You Creator, Your Judgement is the Word

Thank You Creator, The One who delays the punishment for those who deserve it and bless them with forgiveness, if he so wills

Thank You Creator, The One who rewards a lot for a little obedience

Thank You Creator, The One who gives satisfaction

Thank You Creator, The One who protects whatever and whoever He willed to protect

Thank You Creator, The Bountiful One

Thank You Creator, The One who answers the one in need— The Responsive.

Thank You Creator, The Hearkener, The One who rescues the yearned if he calls upon Him

Thank You Creator, The Vast

Thank You Creator, The Judge of judges

Thank You Creator, The One who Resurrects and the Raiser from death

Thank You Creator, The Praised One who deserves to be praised

Thank You Creator, The Originator, The One who created the human being

Thank You Creator, The Restorer, The Giver of life

Thank You Creator, The Creator of death,
The Destroyer

Thank You Creator, The Alive, The One attributed with a life that is unlike our life

Thank You Creator, The Perceiver

Thank You Creator, The One without a partner

Thank You Creator, The One with the perfect Power that nothing is withheld from Him

Thank You Creator, The One who puts things in their right place

Thank You Creator, The One who quickens that He wills and delays that He wills

Thank You Creator, The Source of all Goodness

Thank You Creator, The Eternal owner of Sovereignty

Thank You Creator, The Lord of Majesty and Bounty

Thank You Creator, The Supreme Inheritor

Thank You Creator, The Guide to the Right Path

Thank You Creator, The Purest of the pure

Thank You Creator, The Root of Creation

Thank You Creator, The One who is attained by all

Thank You Creator, The Ever prolific

Thank You Creator, The One worthy of our gratitude

Thank You Creator, The One with All-Embracing Goodness

Thank You Creator, The One with All-Embracing Holy Light

Thank You Creator, The Creator of holy attributes

Thank You Creator, The Fulfiller of holy desires

Thank You Creator, The One who is free

Thank You Creator, The Deliverer from evil

Thank You Creator, The Never deceiving

Thank You Creator, The Never deceived

Thank You Creator, The One without a second

Thank You Creator, His decrees are eternal, unchangeable, holy, wise, and sovereign

Thank You Creator, The Never forgetting

Thank You Creator, The Just Accountant

Thank You Creator, The Creator of life-giving water

Thank You Creator, The Master Craftsman

Thank You Creator, The Rewarder of sincere desires

Thank You Creator, The Creator of all humanity and it's actions

Thank You Creator, The Creator of all human and animal life

Thank You Creator, The Creator of all the five elements

Thank You Creator, The Creator of all the planets and all other worlds

Thank You Creator, The One never in doubt

Thank You Creator, The One eternally awake

Thank You Creator, The Ever alert

Thank You Creator, The Ever protecting

Thank You Creator, The Recorder of Man's actions

Thank You Creator, The Fathomless and Limitless

Thank You Creator, The Awakener of Eternal Spring

Thank You Creator, The One who made the mountains and the seas

Thank You Creator, The One who measured out the universe

Thank You Creator, The One who made the valleys and the skies

Thank You Creator, The One who lit the stars

Thank You Creator, The One who made the darkness and the light

Thank You Creator, The One who made the sun and the moon

Thank You Creator, The One who made the blue skies and the rains

Thank You Creator, The Lord of hope and freedom

Thank You Creator, The Glorious Light beyond all compare

Thank You Creator, The Dispeller of my pains

Thank You Creator, The Pure Intelligence manifested in the universe

Thank You Creator, Who is the Cause of the whole universe and its appearance is His image

Thank You Creator, The Soul Immutable Supreme

Thank You Creator, The Dread of the dreadful

Thank You Creator, The Terror of the terrible

Thank You Creator, The Purifier of all purifiers

Thank You Creator, You alone rule the high-placed ones

Thank You Creator, The imperceptible by the senses, yet the very Truth

Thank You Creator, We worship You alone in our minds

Thank You Creator, We bow to You alone,
the Witness of the universe

Thank You Creator, We seek refuge in the One who is our sole eternal support

Thank You Creator, The Vessel of safety in the ocean of being

Thank You Creator, The One who comes to me in my heart

Thank You Creator, The One who becomes my Inner Voice whenever I ask

Thank You Creator, The Life of my life

Thank You Creator, The Soul of my soul

Thank You Creator, The Homogeneous Essence

Thank You Creator, The Protector of this world

Thank You Creator, The One in the grass and in the rose

Thank You Creator, The Self Luminous

Thank You Creator, My Constant Helper

Thank You Creator, My Loving Protector

Thank You Creator, The One who created the reality of all things out of utter nothingness

Thank You Creator, From nought, You have brought into being the most refined and subtle elements of Your creation

Thank You Creator, The One who rescues creatures from the abasement of remoteness and the perils of ultimate extinction

Thank You Creator, The Lord of Incorruptible Glory

Thank You Creator, The Perfect Embodiment of Integrity

Thank You Creator, The One who possesses awesome glory

Thank You Creator, The One who is fully, always and perfectly purposeful

Thank You Creator, The One who is always in a state of grace.

Thank You Creator, The One who possesses perfection in the timing of anything

Thank You Creator, The One who possesses perfection in the execution of anything

Thank You Creator, The One who is perfectly trustworthy

Thank You Creator, The One who is perfectly faithful

Thank You Creator, The One who possesses complete and perfectly accurate omniscience

Thank You Creator, The One who is consistent

Thank You Creator, The Epitome of empathy

Thank You Creator, The One who is inscrutable

Thank You Creator, The One who is discernible

Thank You Creator, The One who is zealous

Thank You Creator, The One who is fully sufficient to melt all our needs

Thank You Creator, The One who is willing to be angry, wrathful and punishing if need be

Thank You Creator, The Image of the undying

Thank You Creator, The True Primal Beginning

Thank You Creator, The One who is True through the ages

Thank You Creator, True—here, now, and forever true

Thank You Creator, On Your command bodies are created

Thank You Creator, On Your command souls come into being

Thank You Creator, On Your command some are blessed and forgiven

Thank You Creator, On Your command others wander aimlessly forever

Thank You Creator, Everyone is subject to Your command, no one is beyond Your command

Thank You Creator, The Fashioner, who fashions the body and again reduces it to dust

Thank You Creator, The One who takes life away, and then restores it again.

Thank You Creator, The Great Giver who keeps on giving, while those who receive grow weary of receiving

Thank You Creator, The Treasure of Excellence

Thank You Creator, Endless are Your praises

Thank You Creator, Priceless are Your virtues

Thank You Creator, Priceless are Your blessings

Thank You Creator, The One who makes things happen according to the pleasure of His will, such is His celestial order

Thank You Creator, The One who has created the creation and watches over it

Thank You Creator, Whose Glance and Grace bestow happiness

Thank You Creator, Innumerable planets, solar systems and galaxies exist as You command

Thank You Creator, The Righteous Judge of Truth

Thank You Creator, The Master of Unfathomable Depth

Thank You Creator, The True Primal Being

Thank You Creator, The Inaccessible, Unreachable and Unrivalled

Thank You Creator, Everything happens according to Your will

Thank You Creator, Who alone accomplishes all that occurs

Thank You Creator, Whatever pleases You comes to pass

Thank You Creator, Everything that happens is Your doing

Thank You Creator, You are the Imperishable Supreme Being

Thank You Creator, The Inner Knower, the Searcher of hearts

Thank You Creator, The Architect of Destiny

Thank You Creator, None can measure Your worth

Thank You Creator, Wisdom, honour and wealth are showered on those whose hearts are permeated with You

Thank You Creator, The One who is the source of all comfort

Thank You Creator, The One who bestows greatness, eternal Peace, and everlasting joy

Thank You Creator, Your Throne is eternal and immovable

Thank You Creator, The Most Perfect of the perfect

Thank You Creator, The Boat to carry me across the world ocean

Thank You Creator, The Source of Joy

Thank You Creator, The Treasure of liberation

Thank You Creator, The Source of all good fortune

Thank You Creator, The One who is fearless and forever merciful

Thank You Creator, The One who bestows enlightened awareness

Thank You Creator, Who is the support for all and to whom body and soul belong

Thank You Creator, The Truest of the true

Thank You Creator, All things are in Whose power

Thank You Creator, You are immeasurably deep and profound

Thank You Creator, The Hope of all

Thank You Creator, To whom all beings belong

Thank You Creator, You are the Wealth of all

Thank You Creator, Everything is in His hands,
He is the Doer of all deeds

Thank You Creator, The One who is the Knower of all beings

Thank You Creator, The One who is the support of the mind

Thank You Creator, The One who is the support of the breath of life

Thank You Creator, You yourself are in all places and interspaces

Thank You Creator, In Your sanctuary there is eternal peace

Thank You Creator, The Destroyer of pain and suffering of the meek

Thank You Creator, Wondrous is the form of the Immaculate One

Thank You Creator, The Nurturer and the Cherished

Thank You Creator, The deep and profound Ocean of Peace

Thank You Creator, The One Lord is the Doer, the Cause of causes

Thank You Creator, Our Self-sufficient Father

Thank You Creator, The Perfect, the Unseen, the Unknowable

Thank You Creator, The Embodiment of Fulfilment

Thank You Creator, You seek no advice while building, or destroying, while giving or taking

Thank You Creator, You alone know Your Creative Power

Thank You Creator, You yourself do all Your deeds

Thank You Creator, You behold all in Your Vision

Thank You Creator, Greatness is only in Your great hands, You give to those whom You are pleased with

Thank You Creator, The One who unites us to Yourself

Thank You Creator, Whose Value cannot be oppressed

Thank You Creator, The All-compelling

Thank You Creator, Our Lord and Master, the Power of the powerless

Thank You Creator, You created the world, and assigned tasks to one and all

Thank You Creator, You watch over Your creation and through Your All-powerful creative potency You cast the dice

Thank You Creator, The God who is Unity—Single, Whole, Complete Indivisible Entity.

Thank You Creator, You instruct those with whom You are pleased

Thank You Creator, You bestow Your gifts even if we do not ask for them

Thank You Creator, You are the Giver of the fruits of the mind's desires

Thank You Creator, The One who cherishes all beings

Thank You Creator, The One who permeates each and every heart

Thank You Creator, There is only one court of the Creator

Thank You Creator, The Lord's Command is the one and only

Thank You Creator, You delegate the tasks

Thank You Creator, You yourself are pleased beholding Your own Glorious Greatness

Thank You Creator, There is nothing beyond You

Thank You Creator, You yourself are contained in all places

Thank You Creator, You yourself created the earth and the two lamps of the sun and the moon

Thank You Creator, You created the Creative Power of the universe

Thank You Creator, You are the Knower of secrets

Thank You Creator, Great is the Greatness of the Lord

Thank You Creator, Your justice is totally righteous

Thank You Creator, All are Yours and You belong to all

Thank You Creator, You are the Wealth of all

Thank You Creator, Everyone offers prayers to You each day

Thank You Creator, You yourself inspire us to worship You

Thank You Creator, You reveal Your Glorious Greatness

Thank You Creator, You yourself inspire us to place our faith in You

Thank You Creator, The One who alone is Wondrous, no one can describe You

Thank You Creator, The Rejuvenator of the Breath of Life

Thank You Creator, The Subtle Essence of the Lord is the sweetest of all

Thank You Creator, After obtaining Whose favour, the blessed do not waver

Thank You Creator, You transcend all qualities, You possess the Supreme Qualities

Thank You Creator, You are the Giver of peace

Thank You Creator, You are the Enjoyer imbued with love

Thank You Creator, You are the Master, and then again the Servant

Thank You Creator, The entire universe is the arena of Your play

Thank You Creator, All things are Your doing, we can do nothing ourselves

Thank You Creator, The Treasure of Bliss, Joy, Salvation

Thank You Creator, The Intuitive Peace and Poise

Thank You Creator, The Lord has become merciful as it is raining everywhere

Thank You Creator, The Merciful Lord is totally pervading and permeating the water and the land

Thank You Creator, You are merciful to the meek

Thank You Creator, The Ocean of Peace

Thank You Creator, The Supreme Lord is our Protector

Thank You Creator, You give and forgive all beings

Thank You Creator, Contentment, enduring satisfaction and bliss come through the pleasure of Your will

Thank You Creator, The extent of Your Greatness cannot be known

Thank You Creator, The True One abides in my mind and body, all the evildoers and enemies have now become my friends

Thank You Creator, Your Creative Powers and Bounties cannot be described

Thank You Creator, The One who is All-Powerful, Vast, Lofty and Infinite

Thank You Creator, The Source of all Blessings

Thank You Creator, In an instant You establish and disestablish

Thank You Creator, You yourself create, destroy and adorn

Thank You Creator, The joy of all hearts

Thank You Creator, You cause people to act,
You unite with Yourself.

Thank You Creator, The True Author of all the Sacred Teachings

Thank You Creator, You appraise all people, You appraise the true and place them in Your treasury

Thank You Creator, Those who please You are linked to the Truth

Thank You Creator, You are pervading in all forms and colours

Thank You Creator, Praise the One who is ever-present.

Thank You Creator, Who sits deep within the Self

Thank You Creator, There is nothing beyond You, You are the One who sees, knows and does

Thank You Creator, The One who inspires us to work

Thank You Creator, Who is beautiful and who entices the world

Thank You Creator, Who bestows pain and pleasure

Thank You Creator, The Giver of Virtue

Thank You Creator, The Immaculate Lord who bestows Eternal Virtue

Thank You Creator, You yourself lead us to merge in Your Virtuous Goodness

Thank You Creator, Who creates and who beholds

Thank You Creator, The One who created the universe, You alone know it

Thank You Creator, You are the Primal Being—remote and beyond

Thank You Creator, You have no form or shape

Thank You Creator, You are seen within each and every heart

Thank You Creator, You yourself bestow glory on those whom You have so predestined

Thank You Creator, First You created nourishment, then You created the human beings

Thank You Creator, There is no other as Great as You

Thank You Creator, Those who are pleasing to You, meditate on You.

They swim across the worldly sea, and You save them, their ancestors and their families as well.

Thank You Creator, You are EVERYTHING

Thank You Creator, You are Supreme in Omniscience and Goodness, and Unrivalled in Splendour

Thank You Creator, You are my Mountain

Thank You Creator, You are my Shelter and my Shield

Thank You Creator, No one can rival You

Thank You Creator, You protect those who through perfect Destiny merge with You

Thank You Creator, Here and hereafter, You are the Protector

Thank You Creator, In the womb of the mother, You cherish and nurture the baby

Thank You Creator, You are my friend and companion

Thank You Creator, You are Invaluable

Thank You Creator, You are the King,
Your Sovereign Rule is True

Thank You Creator, The Wonder of wonders.

Thank You Creator, When Your Supreme Hand grasps the hand of someone, he shall never again suffer separation from You.

Thank You Creator, You are overflowing with all Powers

Thank You Creator, You are revealed through Your All-powerful creative nature

Thank You Creator, You yourself created and adorned the universe and You yourself complete it

Thank You Creator, The One in Whom the hopes of all rest

Thank You Creator, You yourself are the Appraiser who distinguishes counterfeit from the genuine

Thank You Creator, You are so Great, all greatness flows from You

Thank You Creator, You are so Good, goodness radiates from You

Thank You Creator, You are True, all that flows from You is true

Thank You Creator, You are Infallible, You cannot be fooled

Thank You Creator, As great as You are, so great are Your Gifts. You bestow them according to Your Will.

Thank You Creator, You are the All-powerful Cause of causes

Thank You Creator, The creation is Your subject. You sustain it with Your Mighty Power

Thank You Creator, through faith and trust we receive spiritual wisdom and enlightenment from You

Thank You Creator, By Your grace the Banner of Honour is obtained

Thank You Creator, God of will, God of Grace.

Thank You Creator, The fire of fear within the body is burnt out by the fear of God

Thank You Creator, The fear of God frightens away all other fears

Thank You Creator, The One who created everything, does Everything.

Thank You Creator, Before and after, Your Command is pervading

Thank You Creator, All are Yours, You are the Lord of all

Thank You Creator, You are the True Giver

Thank You Creator, We understand You,
only when You inspire us to understand You

Thank You Creator, He alone knows everything, unto whom You give knowledge

Thank You Creator, The Immortal Lord, whatever You do, comes to pass

Thank You Creator, Those whose hearts are filled with the Lord's Essence are blessed and acclaimed and intuitively absorbed by the Lord

Thank You Creator, We should centre our consciousness firmly on the Lord

Thank You Creator, Those who are imbued with and committed to Your love, are overflowing in abundance. They lack nothing.

Thank You Creator, Day after day, You care for Your beings, the Great Giver, who watches over all.

Thank You Creator, You are the Treasure of Glorious Virtue

Thank You Creator, You are Your own Advisor

Thank You Creator, True is the Lord King, True is Your Royal Command

Thank You Creator, You are the Bestower of Wisdom

Thank You Creator, You have given us all—soul, body, food, shelter, clothing and other pleasures to enjoy

Thank You Creator, This whole play is Yours

Thank You Creator, The Beauty and Light of the Lord is present in all

Thank You Creator, I am in the protection of Your sanctuary

Thank You Creator, You are Your own Master

Thank You Creator, There is no other Giver,
as Great as You are

Thank You Creator, You are merciful,
the Destroyer of all pain

Thank You Creator, The True Lord God who grants forgiveness

Thank You Creator, We are emancipated only when You emancipate us

Thank You Creator, The Lord of the world, Master of the universe, EVERYTHING is under Your control

Thank You Creator, The All-Pervading Lord King,
You are present in every heart

Thank You Creator, You are the Source of Nectar

Thank You Creator, You yourself create, You yourself behold, You yourself assign all their tasks

Thank You Creator, The Supreme Soul is diffused everywhere

Thank You Creator, Your Imminent Presence is pervading everywhere

Thank You Creator, You preserve the honour of Your devotees

Thank You Creator, You are pervading the water, the land and the sky

Thank You Creator, Whatever has been and whatever shall be, comes from You

Thank You Creator, You hold all Your creatures in Your hands and is never separated from them

Thank You Creator, We should abandon all our clever devices and grasp Your support—in an instant, we shall be saved.

Thank You Creator, We should know that You are always Near-at-hand

Thank You Creator, We should accept Your desire as true

Thank You Creator, When You yourself become merciful, the work of Your servant becomes perfect

Thank You Creator, You yourself know Your State and Conditions, how can we describe You!

Thank You Creator, Whatever You attach us to, to that we are attached

Thank You Creator, The Dream is Yours,
the Kingdom is Yours

Thank You Creator, You yourself annihilate, You yourself restore

Thank You Creator, Chanting Your Glorious Praises, our tongue shall become devout

Thank You Creator, You are my Companion,
You are my Best Friend

Thank You Creator, You are my Lord and Master, You are my Leader

Thank You Creator, Your Glory is manifested in each and every heart

Thank You Creator, Remembering You in meditation, sinking stones are made to float

Thank You Creator, After meditating on You, egotism is subdued and the mind does not waver

Thank You Creator, The Saviour, You are the Treasure of Intuitive peace, Poise and Bliss

Thank You Creator, By serving You, all treasures are obtained

Thank You Creator, The Unseen Lord and Master, You are the Treasure of Peace

Thank You Creator, The Supporter of the soul, the Breath of Life

Thank You Creator, Everything is in Your Hands, You are my help and support

Thank You Creator, I have not appreciated all that You have done for me

Thank You Creator, By remembering You in meditation, salvation is attained

Thank You Creator, The Eradicator of evil-mindedness

Thank You Creator, You are the saving Grace of sinners

Thank You Creator, The Master of the masterless

Thank You Creator, You are the Giver of all peace and comfort

Thank You Creator, You yourself instruct those who are misguided when You cast Your Glance of Grace.

Thank You Creator, Praise the Creator, no obstacle will block our mind or body

Thank You Creator, You grant Your Grace

Thank You Creator, the Eradicator of all sorrow

Thank You Creator, By meditating on You, all our sins and terrible mistakes shall be taken away, and we shall be rid of our pride and esteem

Thank You Creator, Whose end and limitations cannot be found

Thank You Creator, Except for You, there is no other at all.

Thank You Creator, whoever knows You in thought, word and deed, becomes just like You

Thank You Creator, You are Fearless

Thank You Creator, You are Invaluable

Thank You Creator, In the fear of God, we enjoy the Fearless Lord

Thank You Creator, The Limitless Primal Lord God

Thank You Creator, The Infinity of the infinite

Thank You Creator, You are the Upholder of the Truth

Thank You Creator, The Personification of Creativity

Thank You Creator, Your Banner of Righteousness waves proudly forever

Thank You Creator, Meditating on You, the wealth of evil-mindedness is washed away

Thank You Creator, To carry humanity across, You bestow Your Radiance

Thank You Creator, The Enlightener of the soul

Thank You Creator, The Self-Illumined Lord

Thank You Creator, Doer of deeds, Cause of causes

Thank You Creator, Singing Your praise, the mind blossoms forth in ecstasy

Thank You Creator, The Undeceivable One

Thank You Creator, The Magic Charm

Thank You Creator, You are the One and Only, no one else is like You

Thank You Creator, You are the Father of the world, the Support of all life

Thank You Creator, Your treasures are unweighable and overflowing in abundance

Thank You Creator, You are the Farthest of the far, Infinite, and Incomparably Bountiful

Thank You Creator, In Your home, creation and destruction happen in an instant

Thank You Creator, Your Light is Immaculate and Pure

Thank You Creator, The world is strung upon Your thread

Thank You Creator, Your Power is unstoppable

Thank You Creator, The cup of loving devotion belongs to You and You give it to whomever You like

Thank You Creator, Our Lord and Master is always here if one remembers Him

Thank You Creator, We should be reverent and humble, whatever happens is what the Creator does

Thank You Creator, You Yourself support the world

Thank You Creator, The Formless,
Formed, Undeceivable,

Perfect, Imperishable, Unchanging,
Blissful, Unlimited, Beautiful,

Immaculate, Blossoming: countless are
Your Glorious Praises

Thank You Creator, The Truest of the true,
the Primal Being, the Primal Soul

Thank You Creator, Sitting upon Your Throne of
Truth, You administer True Justice

Thank You Creator, You fashion the universe,
You are Infallible and do not make mistakes

Thank You Creator, The Priceless Jewel

Thank You Creator, The Inapprehensible Lord

All the praises to You, Our Creator

www.ingramcontent.com/pod-product-compliance
Lightning Source LLC
La Vergne TN
LVHW042344150826
845671LV00001B/9

* 9 7 9 8 8 9 6 9 9 3 7 6 6 *